KITCHEN LIBRARY

Party Food

p

mint & cannellini bean dip

serves six

175 g/6 oz dried cannellini beans

1 small garlic clove, crushed

1 bunch spring onions,
    chopped roughly

handful of fresh mint leaves

2 tbsp tahini

2 tbsp olive oil

1 tsp ground cumin

1 tsp ground coriander

2–3 tbsp lemon juice

salt and pepper

fresh mint sprigs, to garnish

TO SERVE

fresh vegetable crudités, such as
    cauliflower florets, carrots,
    cucumber, radishes and peppers

1 Put the cannellini beans into a bowl and pour over enough cold water to cover. Leave to soak for at least 4 hours or overnight.

2 Drain the beans and rinse under cold water. Put them into a pan and cover with water. Bring to the boil over a high heat and boil rapidly for 10 minutes. Reduce the heat, cover and cook for 1–1½ hours until tender.

3 Drain the beans thoroughly and transfer them to a food processor or bowl. Add the garlic, spring onions, mint, tahini and oil and process the mixture for 15 seconds. Alternatively, mash the ingredients well with a potato masher until smooth.

4 Scrape the mixture into a bowl, if necessary and stir in the spices and enough lemon juice to give a soft consistency. Season to taste with salt and pepper. Mix thoroughly, cover with clingfilm and leave in a cool place, but not the refrigerator, for 30 minutes to allow the flavours to develop fully.

5 Spoon the dip into small serving bowls and garnish with fresh mint sprigs. Put the bowls on to large serving plates and surround them with the prepared vegetable crudités. Serve at room temperature.

tzatziki & black olive dips

serves four

½ cucumber

225 g/8 oz thick natural yogurt

1 tbsp chopped fresh mint

salt and pepper

4 pitta breads

BLACK OLIVE DIP

2 garlic cloves, crushed

125 g/4½ oz stoned black olives

4 tbsp olive oil

2 tbsp lemon juice

1 tbsp chopped fresh parsley

TO GARNISH

1 fresh mint sprig

1 fresh flat-leaf parsley sprig

1 To make the tzatziki, peel the cucumber and chop roughly. Sprinkle with salt and leave to stand for 15–20 minutes. Rinse under cold running water and drain well.

2 Mix the cucumber, yogurt and mint together. Season to taste with salt and pepper and transfer to a serving bowl. Cover and chill in the refrigerator for 20–30 minutes.

3 To make the black olive dip, put the crushed garlic and olives into a food processor or blender and process for about 15–20 seconds. Alternatively, chop them very finely.

4 Add the oil, lemon juice and chopped parsley to the food processor or blender and process for a few more seconds. Alternatively, mix with the garlic and olives and mash together. Season with salt and pepper.

5 Wrap the pitta breads in tinfoil and either put over a hot barbecue for 2–3 minutes, turning once to warm through, or heat in a preheated oven or under a preheated hot grill. Cut into pieces and serve with the tzatziki and black olive dips, garnished with mint and parsley sprigs.

aubergine dipping platter

serves four

1 aubergine, peeled and cut into
   2.5-cm/1-inch cubes
3 tbsp sesame seeds, roasted in a
   dry frying pan over a low heat
1 tsp sesame oil
grated rind and juice of ½ lime
1 small shallot, diced
1 tsp sugar
1 fresh red chilli, deseeded
   and sliced
115 g/4 oz broccoli florets
2 carrots, cut into batons
8 baby sweetcorn, cut in
   half lengthways
2 celery sticks, cut into batons
1 baby red cabbage, cut into
   8 wedges, the leaves of each
   wedge held together by the core
salt and pepper

VARIATION
You can vary the selection
of vegetables depending on
your preference or whatever you
have at hand. Other vegetables
you could use are cauliflower
florets and cucumber batons.

1 Bring a pan of water to the boil over a medium heat. Add the aubergine and cook for 7–8 minutes. Drain well and leave to cool slightly.

2 Meanwhile, grind the sesame seeds with the oil in a food processor or in a mortar with a pestle.

3 Add the aubergine, lime rind and juice, shallot, sugar and chilli to the sesame seeds. Season to taste with salt and pepper, then process until smooth. Alternatively, chop and mash with a potato masher.

4 Adjust the seasoning to taste, then spoon the dip into a bowl.

5 Serve the aubergine dipping platter surrounded by the prepared broccoli, carrots, baby sweetcorn, celery and red cabbage.

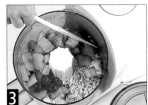

heavenly garlic dip

serves four

2 garlic bulbs

6 tbsp olive oil

1 small onion, chopped finely

2 tbsp lemon juice

3 tbsp tahini

2 tbsp chopped fresh parsley

salt and pepper

1 fresh flat-leaf parsley sprig,
    to garnish

TO SERVE

fresh vegetable crudités

French bread stick or pitta breads

VARIATION

If you come across smoked garlic, use it in this recipe – it tastes wonderful. There is no need to roast the smoked garlic, so omit the first step. This dip can also be used to baste vegetarian burgers.

---

1 Separate the garlic bulbs into individual cloves. Put them on to a baking tray and roast in a preheated oven at 200°C/400°F/Gas Mark 6, for 8–10 minutes. Leave them to cool for a few minutes.

2 When they are cool enough to handle, peel the garlic cloves, then chop finely with a sharp knife.

3 Heat the oil in a frying pan over a low heat. Add the garlic and onion and sauté, stirring occasionally, for 8–10 minutes, or until soft. Remove the pan from the heat.

4 Mix in the lemon juice, tahini and chopped fresh parsley. Season to taste with salt and pepper. Transfer the garlic dip to a small heatproof bowl and keep warm while you prepare the vegetable crudités.

5 When ready to serve, garnish the dip with a fresh parsley sprig and serve with the vegetable crudités, French bread or warmed pitta breads.

paprika crisps

serves four

2 large potatoes
3 tbsp olive oil
½ tsp paprika
salt

1 Slice the potatoes very thinly so that they are almost transparent and place in a bowl of cold water. Drain the potato slices thoroughly and pat dry with kitchen paper.

2 Heat the oil in a large, heavy-based frying pan and add the paprika. Cook, stirring constantly to ensure that the paprika doesn't catch on the base and burn.

3 Add the potato slices to the frying pan and cook them in a single layer over a medium-low heat for about 5 minutes, or until the potato slices are just beginning to curl slightly at the edges.

4 Remove the potato slices from the pan using a slotted spoon and transfer them to kitchen paper to drain thoroughly.

5 Thread the potato slices on to several wooden kebab skewers.

6 Sprinkle the potato slices with salt and cook over a medium hot barbecue or under a medium grill, turning frequently, for 10 minutes, until they begin to go crisp. Sprinkle with a little more salt and serve immediately.

chinese potato crisps

serves four

650 g/1 lb 7 oz medium potatoes

125 ml/4 fl oz vegetable oil

1 fresh red chilli, halved
    and deseeded

1 small onion, quartered

2 garlic cloves, halved

2 tbsp light soy sauce

pinch of salt

1 tsp wine vinegar

1 tbsp coarse sea salt

pinch of chilli powder

1 Peel the potatoes and cut into thin slices along their length. Cut the slices into matchsticks.

2 Bring a saucepan of water to the boil and blanch the potato sticks for 2 minutes, drain, rinse under cold water and drain well again. Pat the potato sticks thoroughly dry with absorbent kitchen paper.

3 Heat the oil in a preheated wok until it is almost smoking. Add the chilli, onion and garlic and stir-fry for 30 seconds. Remove and discard the chilli, onion and garlic.

4 Add the potato sticks to the oil and fry for 3–4 minutes, or until golden all over.

5 Add the soy sauce, salt and vinegar to the wok, reduce the heat and cook for 1 minute, or until the potatoes are crisp.

6 Remove the potatoes with a slotted spoon and drain on absorbent kitchen paper.

7 Transfer the potato sticks to a serving dish, sprinkle with the sea salt and chilli powder and serve.

sesame prawn toasts

serves four

225 g/8 oz peeled cooked prawns

1 spring onion

¼ tsp salt

1 tsp light soy sauce

1 tbsp cornflour

1 egg white, beaten

3 thin slices white bread,
   crusts removed

4 tbsp sesame seeds

vegetable oil, for deep-frying

COOK'S TIP

Fry the triangles in 2 batches,
keeping the first batch warm
while you cook the second, to
prevent them from sticking
together and overcooking.

2 Spread the mixture on to one side of each slice of bread. Spread the sesame seeds on top of the mixture, pressing down well.

1 Put the prawns and spring onion in a food processor and process until finely minced. Alternatively, chop them very finely. Transfer to a bowl and stir in the salt, soy sauce, cornflour and egg white.

3 Cut each slice into 4 equal triangles or strips.

4 Heat the oil for deep-frying in a wok until almost smoking. Carefully place the triangles in the oil, coated side down, and cook for 2–3 minutes, until golden brown. Remove with a slotted spoon and drain on kitchen paper. Serve hot.

vegetable kebabs

makes twelve

600 g/1 lb 5 oz potatoes, sliced

1 medium onion, sliced

½ medium cauliflower, cut into
    small florets

50 g/1¾ oz cooked peas

1 tbsp spinach purée

2–3 fresh green chillies

1 tbsp fresh coriander leaves

1 tsp finely chopped fresh
    root ginger

1 tsp crushed garlic

1 tsp ground coriander

pinch of ground turmeric

1 tsp salt

50 g/1¾ oz breadcrumbs

300 ml/10 fl oz vegetable oil

fresh chilli strips, to garnish

1 Place the potatoes, onion and cauliflower florets in a large pan of water and bring to the boil. Reduce the heat and simmer gently until the potatoes are cooked through and tender. Remove the vegetables from the pan with a slotted spoon and drain thoroughly. Reserve.

2 Add the peas and spinach to the vegetables and mix, mashing down thoroughly with a fork.

3 Using a sharp knife, finely chop the green chillies and the fresh coriander leaves.

4 Mix the green chillies and fresh coriander leaves with the ginger, garlic, ground coriander, ground turmeric and salt.

5 Blend the spice mixture into the vegetables, mixing with a fork to make a paste.

6 Scatter the breadcrumbs on to a large plate.

7 Break off 10–12 small balls from the spice paste. Flatten them with the palm of your hand or with a palette knife to make flat, round shapes.

8 Dip each kebab in the breadcrumbs, coating well.

9 Heat the oil in a heavy-based frying-pan and fry the kebabs, in batches, until golden brown, turning occasionally. Transfer to serving plates and garnish with fresh chilli strips. Serve hot.

onion tart

serves four

250 g/9 oz ready-made shortcrust
   pastry, thawed if frozen
plain flour, for dusting
3 tbsp butter
75 g/2¾ oz bacon, chopped
700 g/1 lb 9 oz onions, sliced thinly
2 eggs, beaten
50 g/1¾ oz freshly grated
   Parmesan cheese
1 tsp dried sage
salt and pepper

VARIATION

To make a vegetarian version
of this tart, replace the bacon
with the same amount of
chopped mushrooms.

1 Roll out the pastry on a lightly
floured work surface and use it to
line a 24-cm/9½-inch loose-bottomed
quiche or flan tin.

2 Prick the base of the pastry with a
fork and chill in the refrigerator for
30 minutes.

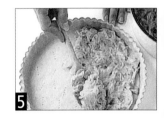

3 Meanwhile, heat the butter in
a saucepan, add the bacon and
onions and sweat over a low heat for
about 25 minutes, or until tender. If
the onion slices start to brown, add
1 tablespoon of water to the saucepan.

4 Add the beaten eggs to the onion
mixture and stir in the Parmesan
cheese and sage. Season with salt and
pepper to taste.

5 Spoon the mixture into the
prepared pastry case.

6 Bake in a preheated oven,
180°C/350°F/Gas Mark 4, for
20–30 minutes, or until the onion
filling has just set and the pastry is
crisp and golden.

7 Leave in the tin to cool slightly.
Serve warm or cold.

mini cheese & onion tarts

makes twelve

PASTRY

100 g/3½ oz plain flour, plus extra
    for dusting

¼ tsp salt

5½ tbsp butter, diced

1–2 tbsp water

FILLING

1 egg, beaten

100 ml/3½ fl oz single cream

50 g/1¾ oz Red Leicester
    cheese, grated

3 spring onions, chopped finely

salt

cayenne pepper

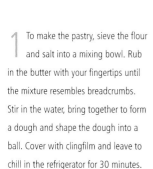

1 To make the pastry, sieve the flour and salt into a mixing bowl. Rub in the butter with your fingertips until the mixture resembles breadcrumbs. Stir in the water, bring together to form a dough and shape the dough into a ball. Cover with clingfilm and leave to chill in the refrigerator for 30 minutes.

2 Roll out the dough on a lightly floured work surface. Stamp out 12 rounds from the pastry using a 7.5-cm/3-inch biscuit cutter, and use them to line a tartlet tin.

3 To make the filling, whisk the beaten egg, cream, Red Leicester cheese and spring onions together in a jug. Season to taste with salt and cayenne pepper.

4 Pour the filling into the pastry cases and bake in a preheated oven, 180°C/350°F/Gas Mark 4, for about 20–25 minutes, or until the filling is just set and the pastry is golden brown. Transfer the tartlets to a warmed serving platter if serving warm, or to a wire rack to cool if serving cold.

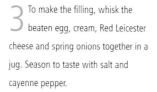

goat's cheese, pear & walnut salad

serves four

250 g/9 oz dried penne

1 head radicchio, torn into pieces

1 Webbs lettuce, torn into pieces

7 tbsp chopped walnuts

2 ripe pears, cored and diced

1 bunch watercress, trimmed

2 tbsp lemon juice

5 tbsp olive oil

1 garlic clove, chopped

3 tbsp white wine vinegar

4 tomatoes, quartered

1 small onion, sliced

1 large carrot, grated

250 g/9 oz goat's cheese, diced

salt and pepper

COOK'S TIP

Most goat's cheese comes from France and there are many varieties, such as Crottin de Chavignol, Chabi, which is very pungent and Sainte-Maure, which is available in creamery and farmhouse varieties.

---

1 Bring a large pan of lightly salted water to the boil over a medium heat. Add the pasta and cook for about 8–10 minutes, or until tender, but still firm to the bite. Drain the pasta, refresh under cold running water, drain again and leave to cool.

2 Put the radicchio and Webbs lettuce into a large salad bowl and mix together well. Top with the pasta, walnuts, pears and watercress.

3 Mix the lemon juice, oil, garlic and vinegar together in a measuring jug. Pour the mixture over the salad ingredients and toss to coat the salad leaves thoroughly.

4 Add the tomato quarters, onion slices, grated carrot and diced goat's cheese and, using 2 forks, toss together until well mixed. Leave the salad to chill in the refrigerator for about 1 hour before serving.

chicken or beef satay

4 boneless, skinned chicken breasts
  or 750 g/1 lb 10 oz rump
  steak, trimmed

lime wedges, to serve

MARINADE

1 small onion, chopped finely

1 garlic clove, crushed

2.5-cm/1-inch piece fresh root
  ginger, grated

2 tbsp dark soy sauce

2 tsp chilli powder

1 tsp ground coriander

2 tsp dark brown sugar

1 tbsp lemon or lime juice

1 tbsp vegetable oil

SAUCE

300 ml/10 fl oz coconut milk

4 tbsp crunchy peanut butter

1 tbsp fish sauce

1 tsp lemon or lime juice

salt and pepper

1 Using a sharp knife, trim any fat from the chicken or beef and discard. Cut the meat into thin strips, about 7.5-cm/3-inches long.

2 To make the marinade, put all the ingredients into a shallow dish and mix well. Add the meat strips and coat well in the marinade. Cover with clingfilm and leave to marinate in the refrigerator for at least 2 hours, or preferably overnight.

3 Remove the meat from the marinade and thread the pieces, concertina style, on to presoaked bamboo or thin wooden skewers.

4 Put the satays under a preheated medium-hot grill and cook for 8–10 minutes, turning and brushing occasionally with the marinade until cooked through.

5 To make the sauce, mix the coconut milk with the peanut butter, fish sauce and lemon juice in a pan. Bring to the boil and cook for 3 minutes. Season with salt and pepper.

6 Pour the sauce into a bowl and serve with the satays and lime.

meatballs in spicy sauce

serves four

225 g/8 oz floury potatoes, diced

225 g/8 oz beef or lamb mince

1 onion, chopped finely

1 tbsp chopped fresh coriander

1 celery stick, chopped finely

2 garlic cloves, crushed

2 tbsp butter

1 tbsp vegetable oil

salt and pepper

chopped fresh coriander, to garnish

SAUCE

1 tbsp vegetable oil

1 onion, chopped finely

2 tsp soft brown sugar

400 g/14 oz canned
    chopped tomatoes

1 fresh green chilli, deseeded
    and chopped

1 tsp paprika

150 ml/5 fl oz vegetable stock

2 tsp cornflour

1 Cook the diced potatoes in a saucepan of boiling water for 25 minutes, until cooked through. Drain well and transfer to a large mixing bowl. Mash until smooth.

2 Add the beef or lamb mince, onion, coriander, celery, garlic and seasoning and mix together well.

3 Bring the mixture together with your hands and roll it into 20 small balls.

4 To make the sauce, heat the oil in a pan and sauté the onion for 5 minutes. Add the remaining sauce ingredients and bring to the boil, stirring constantly. Lower the heat and simmer for 20 minutes.

5 Meanwhile, heat the butter and oil for the meatballs in a frying pan. Add the meatballs, in batches, and cook, turning frequently, for

10–15 minutes, until browned. Keep warm while cooking the remainder. Transfer the meatballs to a warm, shallow dish and serve with the sauce poured around them and garnished with the fresh coriander.

hummus & garlic toasts

serves four

400 g/14 oz canned chickpeas

juice of 1 large lemon

6 tbsp tahini

2 tbsp olive oil

2 garlic cloves, crushed

salt and pepper

GARLIC TOASTS

1 ciabatta loaf, sliced

2 garlic cloves, crushed

1 tbsp chopped fresh coriander

4 tbsp olive oil

TO GARNISH

1 tbsp chopped fresh coriander

6 stoned black olives

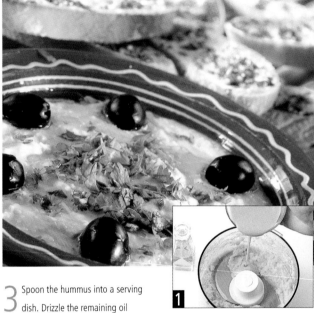

1 To make the hummus, firstly drain the chickpeas, reserving about 2–3 tablespoons of the liquid. Put the chickpeas and half the liquid into a food processor and blend, gradually adding the remaining liquid and lemon juice. Blend well after each addition until smooth.

2 Stir in the tahini and all but 1 teaspoon of the oil. Add the garlic, season to taste with salt and pepper and blend again until smooth.

3 Spoon the hummus into a serving dish. Drizzle the remaining oil over the top and chill in the refrigerator.

4 To make the garlic toasts, lay the slices of ciabatta on a grill rack in a single layer.

5 Mix the garlic, coriander and oil together and drizzle over the bread. Cook under a preheated medium-hot grill for 2–3 minutes until golden, turning once. To serve, garnish the hummus with chopped coriander and olives, then serve with the toasts.

oriental shellfish kebabs

serves twelve

350 g/12 oz raw tiger prawns,
   peeled, leaving tails intact
350 g/12 oz scallops, cleaned,
   trimmed and halved (quartered
   if large)
1 bunch spring onions, sliced into
   2.5-cm/1-inch pieces
1 medium red pepper, deseeded
   and cubed
100 g/3½ oz baby sweetcorn,
   trimmed and sliced into
   1-cm/½-inch pieces
3 tbsp dark soy sauce
½ tsp hot chilli powder
½ tsp ground ginger
1 tbsp sunflower oil
DIP
4 tbsp dark soy sauce
4 tbsp dry sherry
2 tsp clear honey
2.5-cm/1-inch piece fresh root
   ginger, grated
1 spring onion, trimmed and very
   finely sliced

1 Soak 12 wooden skewers in warm water for at least 30 minutes before you use them to prevent the skewers burning. Divide the prawns, scallops, spring onions, pepper and baby sweetcorn into 12 portions and thread on to the skewers. Cover the ends of each with a piece of tinfoil and put into a large shallow dish.

2 Mix the soy sauce, chilli powder and ground ginger together and use to coat the kebabs. Cover and chill in the refrigerator for about 2 hours.

3 Arrange the kebabs on a grill rack. Brush with the oil and cook under a preheated hot grill for about 2–3 minutes on each side until the prawns turn pink, the scallops become opaque and the vegetables are soft.

4 Mix the dip ingredients together in a small bowl and reserve.

5 Remove the tinfoil from the ends of the kebabs and transfer to a warmed serving platter and serve immediately with the dip.

chicken balls with dipping sauce

serves four

2 large skinless, boneless chicken
 breast portions

3 tbsp vegetable oil

2 shallots, chopped finely

½ celery stick, chopped finely

1 garlic clove, crushed

2 tbsp light soy sauce

1 small egg, beaten lightly

1 bunch of spring onions

salt and pepper

spring onion tassels, to garnish

DIPPING SAUCE

3 tbsp dark soy sauce

1 tbsp rice wine

1 tsp sesame seeds

1 Cut the chicken into 2-cm/¾-inch pieces. Heat half of the oil in a preheated wok or frying pan and stir-fry the chicken over a high heat for about 2–3 minutes, until golden. Remove from the wok or pan with a slotted spoon and reserve.

2 Add the shallots, celery and garlic to the wok or pan and stir-fry for 1–2 minutes, until softened.

3 Place the chicken, shallots, celery and garlic in a food processor and process until finely minced. Add 1 tablespoon of the light soy sauce and just enough egg to make a fairly firm mixture. Season to taste with salt and pepper.

4 Trim the spring onions and cut into 5-cm/2-inch lengths. Make the dipping sauce by mixing together the dark soy sauce, rice wine and sesame seeds in a small serving bowl and reserve.

5 Shape the chicken mixture into 16–18 walnut-size balls. Heat the remaining oil in the wok or frying pan and stir-fry the chicken balls, in small batches, for 4–5 minutes, until golden brown. As each batch is cooked, drain on kitchen paper and keep hot.

6 Add the spring onions to the wok or pan and stir-fry for 1–2 minutes, until they begin to soften, then stir in the remaining light soy sauce. Serve with the chicken balls and the bowl of dipping sauce on a platter, garnished with the spring onion tassels.

lentil pâté

serves four

1 tbsp vegetable oil, plus extra
   for greasing
1 onion, chopped
2 garlic cloves, crushed
1 tsp garam masala
½ tsp ground coriander
850 ml/1½ pints vegetable stock
175 g/6 oz red split lentils
1 small egg
2 tbsp milk
2 tbsp mango chutney
2 tbsp chopped fresh parsley
fresh parsley sprigs, to garnish
TO SERVE
salad leaves
warm toast

VARIATION

Use other spices, such as chilli
powder or Chinese five-spice
powder to flavour the pâté and
add tomato relish or chilli relish
instead of the mango chutney,
if you prefer.

1 Heat the oil in a large pan over a medium heat. Add the onion and garlic and sauté for 2–3 minutes, stirring constantly. Add the spices and cook for a further 30 seconds. Stir in the stock and lentils and bring the mixture to the boil. Reduce the heat and simmer for 20 minutes, or until the lentils are cooked. Remove from the heat and drain off any excess moisture.

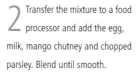

2 Transfer the mixture to a food processor and add the egg, milk, mango chutney and chopped parsley. Blend until smooth.

3 Grease and line the base of a 450 g/1 lb loaf tin. Spoon the mixture into the tin and level the surface. Cover and cook in a preheated oven at 200°C/400°F/Gas Mark 6, for 40–45 minutes, or until firm.

4 Leave the pâté to cool in the tin for 20 minutes, then transfer to the refrigerator to cool completely. Turn out on to a serving plate, garnish with fresh parsley sprigs and serve in slices with salad leaves and warm toast.

mixed bean pâté

serves four

400 g/14 oz canned mixed
  beans, drained
2 tbsp olive oil
juice of 1 lemon
2 garlic cloves, crushed
1 tbsp chopped fresh coriander
2 spring onions, chopped
salt and pepper
shredded spring onions,
  to garnish

1 Rinse the mixed beans thoroughly under cold running water and drain thoroughly.

2 Transfer the beans to a food processor or blender and process until smooth. Alternatively, put the beans into a bowl and mash by hand with a fork or potato masher.

3 Add the oil, lemon juice, garlic, chopped coriander and spring onions and blend until fairly smooth. Season to taste with salt and pepper.

4 Transfer the pâté to a serving bowl, cover and chill in the refrigerator for at least 30 minutes.

5 Garnish with shredded spring onions and serve immediately.

vegetable spring rolls

serves four

225 g/8 oz carrots

1 red pepper

1 tbsp sunflower oil, plus extra
    for frying

75 g/2¾ oz beansprouts

finely grated rind and juice of 1 lime

1 fresh red chilli, deseeded and
    finely chopped

1 tbsp light soy sauce

½ tsp arrowroot

2 tbsp chopped fresh coriander

8 sheets filo pastry

2 tbsp butter

2 tsp sesame oil

TO SERVE

spring onion tassels

chilli sauce

1 Using a sharp knife, cut the carrots into thin sticks. Deseed the pepper and cut into thin slices.

2 Heat the sunflower oil in a large preheated wok.

3 Add the carrot, red pepper and beansprouts and cook, stirring, for 2 minutes, or until softened. Remove the wok from the heat and toss in the lime rind and juice, and the red chilli.

4 Mix the soy sauce with the arrowroot to a smooth paste. Stir the mixture into the wok, return to the heat and cook for 2 minutes, or until the juices thicken.

5 Add the chopped fresh coriander to the wok and mix well, then remove the wok from the heat.

6 Lay the sheets of filo pastry out on a board. Melt the butter with the sesame oil and brush each sheet with the mixture.

7 Spoon a little of the vegetable filling on to the top of each sheet, fold over each long side, and roll up.

8 Add a little oil to the wok and cook the spring rolls, in batches, for 2–3 minutes, or until crisp and golden brown.

9 Transfer the spring rolls to a serving dish, garnish with the spring onion tassels and serve hot with chilli dipping sauce.

spicy potato fries

serves four

4 large waxy potatoes

2 sweet potatoes

4 tbsp butter, melted

½ tsp chilli powder

1 tsp garam masala

salt

COOK'S TIP

Rinsing the potatoes in cold water before cooking removes the starch, thus preventing them from sticking together. Soaking the potatoes in cold salted water makes the cooked chips crisper.

1 Cut both the potatoes and sweet potatoes into slices about 1-cm/½-inch thick, then cut them into finger-shaped chips.

2 Place the potatoes in a large bowl of cold salted water. Leave to soak for 20 minutes.

3 Remove the potato slices with a slotted spoon and drain thoroughly. Pat with kitchen paper until they are completely dry.

4 Pour the melted butter on to a baking tray. Transfer the potato slices to the baking tray.

5 Sprinkle with the chilli powder and garam masala, turning the potato slices to coat them with the spice mixture.

6 Cook the chips in a preheated oven, 200°C/400°F/Gas Mark 6, turning frequently, for 40 minutes, until browned and cooked through.

7 Drain the fries well on kitchen paper to remove the excess oil and serve immediately.

lentil & red pepper flan

serves six

PASTRY

225 g/8 oz plain wholemeal flour,
    plus extra for dusting

100 g/3½ oz vegan
    margarine, diced

4 tbsp water

FILLING

175 g/6 oz red lentils, rinsed

300 ml/10 fl oz vegetable stock

1 tbsp vegan margarine

1 onion, chopped

2 red peppers, deseeded and diced

1 tsp yeast extract

1 tbsp tomato purée

3 tbsp chopped fresh parsley

pepper

1 To make the pastry, sieve the flour into a mixing bowl and add any bran remaining in the sieve. Add the margarine and rub in with your fingertips until the mixture resembles fine breadcrumbs. Stir in the water and bring together to form a dough. Wrap in clingfilm and chill in the refrigerator for 30 minutes.

2 Meanwhile, to make the filling, put the lentils in a saucepan with the stock, bring to the boil, then simmer for 10 minutes, until the lentils are tender. Remove from the heat and mash the lentils into a purée.

3 Melt the margarine in a small frying pan over a low heat, add the onion and red peppers and cook for about 3 minutes, until just soft.

4 Add the lentil purée, yeast extract, tomato purée and parsley. Season to taste with pepper. Mix until thoroughly blended.

5 Roll out the dough on a lightly floured work surface and use it to line a 24-cm/9½-inch loose-bottomed quiche or flan tin. Prick the base of the pastry with a fork and spoon the lentil mixture into the pastry case.

6 Bake in a preheated oven, 200°C/400°F/Gas Mark 6, for 30 minutes, until the filling is set.

spicy pork balls

serves four

450 g/1 lb pork mince

2 shallots, chopped finely

2 garlic cloves, crushed

1 tsp cumin seeds

½ tsp chilli powder

25 g/1 oz wholemeal
    breadcrumbs

1 egg, beaten

2 tbsp sunflower oil

400 g/14 oz canned chopped
    tomatoes, flavoured with chilli

2 tbsp soy sauce

200 g/7 oz canned water chestnuts,
    drained and rinsed

3 tbsp chopped fresh coriander

COOK'S TIP

Add a few teaspoons of chilli
sauce to a can of chopped
tomatoes, if you can't find the
flavoured variety.

1 Place the pork mince in a large mixing bowl. Add the shallots, garlic, cumin seeds, chilli powder, breadcrumbs and beaten egg and mix together well.

2 Form the mixture into small balls between the dampened palms of your hands.

3 Heat the oil in a large preheated wok or heavy-based frying pan. Add the pork balls and stir-fry, in batches, over a high heat for about 5 minutes, or until sealed on all sides.

4 Add the tomatoes, soy sauce and water chestnuts and bring to the boil. Return the pork balls to the wok, reduce the heat and simmer gently for 15 minutes.

5 Scatter with chopped fresh coriander and serve hot.

creamy stuffed mushrooms

serves four

25 g/1 oz dried ceps

225 g/8 oz floury potatoes, diced

2 tbsp butter, melted

4 tbsp double cream

2 tbsp snipped fresh chives

8 large open-capped mushrooms

25 g/1 oz Emmenthal
   cheese, grated

150 ml/5 fl oz vegetable stock

salt and pepper

fresh chives, to garnish

VARIATION

Use fresh mushrooms instead of the dried ceps, if preferred, and stir a mixture of chopped nuts into the mushroom stuffing mixture for extra crunch.

1 Place the dried ceps in a small bowl. Add sufficient boiling water to cover and leave to soak for 20 minutes.

2 Meanwhile, cook the potatoes in a medium saucepan of lightly salted, boiling water for 10 minutes, until cooked through and tender. Drain well and mash until smooth.

3 Drain the soaked ceps and then chop them finely. Mix them into the mashed potato.

4 Thoroughly blend the butter, cream and snipped fresh chives together and pour the mixture into the ceps and potato mixture, mixing well. Season to taste with salt and pepper.

5 Remove the stalks from the open-capped mushrooms. Chop the stalks and stir them into the potato mixture. Spoon the mixture into the open-capped mushrooms and sprinkle the cheese over the top.

6 Arrange the filled mushrooms in a shallow ovenproof dish and pour in the vegetable stock.

7 Cover the dish and cook in a preheated oven, 220°C/425°F/Gas Mark 7, for 20 minutes. Remove the lid and cook for a further 5 minutes, until golden. Serve the mushrooms immediately, garnished with chives.

smoked fish & potato pâté

650 g/1 lb 7 oz floury potatoes,
    peeled and diced
300 g/10½ oz smoked mackerel,
    skinned and flaked
75 g/2¾ oz cooked gooseberries
2 tsp lemon juice
2 tbsp low-fat crème fraîche
1 tbsp capers
1 gherkin, chopped
1 tbsp chopped pickled
    dill cucumber
1 tbsp chopped fresh dill
salt and pepper
lemon wedges, to garnish
toast or warm crusty bread, to serve

COOK'S TIP
Use stewed, canned or
bottled cooked gooseberries
for convenience and to
save time, or when fresh
gooseberries are out of season.

1 Bring a large pan of water to the boil over a medium heat. Add the potatoes and cook for 10 minutes, or until tender, then drain thoroughly.

2 Put the cooked potatoes into a food processor or blender. Add the skinned and flaked smoked mackerel and process for 30 seconds until fairly smooth. Alternatively, put the ingredients into a large bowl and mash with a fork.

3 Add the cooked gooseberries, lemon juice and crème fraîche to the fish and potato mixture. Blend for a further 10 seconds or mash well.

4 Stir in the capers, gherkin, dill cucumber and fresh dill. Season well with salt and pepper.

5 Transfer the pâté to a serving dish and garnish with lemon wedges. Serve with slices of toast or warm crusty bread cut into chunks or slices.

pork sesame toasts

serves four

250 g/9 oz lean pork

250 g/9 oz raw, prawns, peeled and deveined

4 spring onions, trimmed

1 garlic clove, crushed

1 tbsp chopped fresh coriander leaves and stems

1 tbsp fish sauce

1 egg, beaten

8–10 slices of thick-cut white bread

3 tbsp sesame seeds

150 ml/5 fl oz vegetable oil

salt and pepper

TO GARNISH

fresh coriander sprigs

½ red pepper, sliced finely

1 Put the pork, prawns, spring onions, garlic, chopped coriander, fish sauce and the egg into a food processor or blender. Season with salt and pepper and process for a few seconds until finely chopped. Transfer the mixture to a bowl. Alternatively, chop the pork, prawns and spring onions very finely, then add the garlic, chopped coriander, fish sauce and beaten egg. Season with salt and pepper and mix until blended.

2 Spread the pork and prawn mixture thickly over the slices of bread so it reaches up to the edges. Cut off the crusts and slice each piece of bread into 4 squares or triangles.

3 Sprinkle the topping liberally with sesame seeds.

4 Heat a large wok over a medium heat. Add the oil and when hot, fry a few pieces of the bread, topping side down first so the egg sets, for about 2 minutes or until golden. Turn the pieces over to cook on the other side, about 1 minute.

5 Remove the toasts from the wok and drain on kitchen paper. Fry the remaining pieces. Arrange the toasts on a serving plate, garnish with a few fresh coriander sprigs and slices of red pepper and serve.

potato & pepperoni pizza

serves four

1 tbsp butter, plus extra for greasing

plain flour, for dusting

900 g/2 lb floury potatoes, diced

1 tbsp butter

2 garlic cloves, crushed

2 tbsp chopped mixed fresh herbs

1 egg, beaten

6 tbsp passata

2 tbsp tomato purée

50 g/1¾ oz pepperoni slices

1 green pepper, deseeded and
    cut into strips

1 yellow pepper, deseeded and
    cut into strips

2 large open-cap mushrooms, sliced

25 g/1 oz stoned black olives,
    quartered

125 g/4½ oz mozzarella
    cheese, sliced

preheated oven, 220°C/425°F/Gas
Mark 7, for 7–10 minutes, until set.

3 Mix the passata and tomato
purée together and spoon it over
the pizza base, to within 1-cm/½-inch
of the edge of the base.

4 Arrange the pepperoni slices and
the peppers, mushrooms and
olives on top of the passata.

5 Scatter the mozzarella cheese
on top of the pizza. Return to the
oven for 20 minutes, or until the base
is cooked through and the cheese has
melted on top. Serve hot.

1 Grease and flour a 23-cm/9-inch
pizza pan. Cook the potatoes in a
pan of boiling water for 10 minutes, or
until tender. Drain and mash, then
transfer to a mixing bowl and stir in the
butter, garlic, herbs and egg.

2 Spread the mixture into the
prepared pizza pan. Cook in a

35

mexican-style pizzas

serves four

4 ready-made individual pizza bases

1 tbsp olive oil

200 g/7 oz canned chopped
  tomatoes with garlic and herbs

2 tbsp tomato purée

200 g/7 oz canned kidney beans,
  drained and rinsed

115 g/4 oz sweetcorn kernels,
  thawed if frozen

1–2 tsp chilli sauce

1 large red onion, shredded

100 g/3½ oz mature Cheddar
  cheese, grated

1 large, fresh green chilli, deseeded
  and sliced into rings

salt and pepper

COOK'S TIP

Serve a Mexican-style salad
with this pizza. Arrange sliced
tomatoes, fresh coriander leaves
and a few slices of a small,
ripe avocado on a platter.
Sprinkle with fresh lime juice
and coarse sea salt.

1 Arrange the ready-made pizza
bases on a large baking tray
and brush the surfaces lightly with
the olive oil.

2 Mix the chopped tomatoes,
tomato purée, kidney beans and
sweetcorn together in a bowl and
add chilli sauce to taste. Season with
salt and pepper.

3 Spread the tomato and kidney
bean mixture evenly over each
of the pizza bases.

4 Top each pizza with shredded
onion and sprinkle with some
grated Cheddar cheese and a few
slices of green chilli, to taste.

5 Bake in a preheated oven, 220°C/
425°F/Gas Mark 7, for about
20 minutes, until the vegetables are
tender, the cheese has melted and the
base is crisp and golden.

6 Remove the pizzas from the
baking tray and transfer to
serving plates. Serve hot.

crostini alla fiorentina

serves four

3 tbsp olive oil

1 onion, chopped

1 celery stick, chopped

1 carrot, chopped

1–2 garlic cloves, crushed

125 g/4½ oz chicken livers

125 g/4½ oz calf's, lamb's or
   pig's liver

150 ml/5 fl oz red wine

1 tbsp tomato purée

2 tbsp chopped fresh parsley

3–4 canned anchovy fillets,
   chopped finely

2 tbsp stock or water

25–40 g/1–1½ oz butter

1 tbsp capers

salt and pepper

chopped fresh parsley, to garnish

toasted bread, to serve

1 Heat the oil in a frying pan over a low heat. Add the onion, celery, carrot and garlic and cook for about 4–5 minutes, or until the onion is soft.

2 Rinse the chicken livers and pat dry on kitchen paper. Rinse the calf's or other liver and pat dry. Slice into strips. Add the liver to the pan and fry for a few minutes until the strips are well sealed on all sides.

3 Add half the wine and cook until it has mostly evaporated. Add the rest of the wine, tomato purée, half the parsley, anchovy fillets, stock or water, a little salt and plenty of pepper.

4 Cover the pan and simmer, stirring occasionally, for about 15–20 minutes, or until tender and most of the liquid has been absorbed.

5 Leave the mixture to cool slightly, then either coarsely mince or put into a food processor and process to a chunky purée.

6 Return to the pan and add the butter, capers and remaining parsley. Heat through gently until the butter melts. Adjust the seasoning, if necessary and spoon into a bowl. Garnish with chopped parsley and serve warm or cold spread on slices of toasted bread.

onion & mozzarella tarts

serves four

250 g/9 oz puff pastry, thawed
   if frozen
plain flour, for dusting
2 red onions
1 red pepper
8 cherry tomatoes, halved
100g/3½ oz mozzarella cheese,
   cut into chunks
8 fresh thyme sprigs

1 Roll out the pastry on a lightly floured work surface to make 4 squares, 7.5 cm/3 inches wide. Trim the edges of the pastry using a sharp knife, reserving the trimmings. Chill in the refrigerator for 30 minutes.

2 Place the pastry squares on a baking tray. Brush a little water around the edges of the pastry squares and use the reserved pastry trimmings to make a rim around each tart.

3 Cut the red onions into thin wedges and halve and deseed the red pepper.

4 Place the onions and red pepper in a grill pan. Cook under a preheated medium grill for 15 minutes, or until charred.

5 Place the roasted pepper halves in a polythene bag and leave to sweat for 10 minutes. When the pepper is cool enough to handle, peel off the skin and cut the flesh into strips.

6 Line the pastry squares with squares of foil. Bake in a preheated oven, 200°C/400°F/Gas Mark 6 for 10 minutes. Remove and discard the foil and bake the tart cases for a further 5 minutes.

7 Divide the onions, pepper strips, tomatoes and cheese between the tarts and sprinkle with fresh thyme.

8 Bake for a further 15 minutes, or until the pastry is golden. Transfer to warmed serving plates if serving hot, or to a wire rack to cool, if serving cold.

vegetable samosas

makes twelve

FILLING

2 tbsp vegetable oil

1 onion, chopped

½ tsp ground coriander

½ tsp ground cumin

pinch of ground turmeric

½ tsp ground ginger

½ tsp garam masala

1 garlic clove, crushed

225 g/8 oz potatoes, diced

100 g/3½ oz frozen peas, thawed

150 g/5½ oz spinach, chopped

lemon wedges to garnish

PASTRY

350 g/12 oz (12 sheets) filo pastry

oil, for deep-frying

1 To make the filling, heat the oil in a frying pan. Add the onion and sauté, stirring frequently, for 1–2 minutes, until softened. Stir in all of the spices and garlic and cook for 1 minute.

2 Add the potatoes and cook over a low heat, stirring frequently, for 5 minutes, until they begin to soften.

3 Stir in the peas and spinach and cook for a further 3–4 minutes.

4 Lay the filo pastry sheets out on a clean work surface and fold each sheet in half lengthways.

5 Place 2 tablespoons of the vegetable filling at one end of each folded pastry sheet. Fold over one corner to make a triangle. Continue folding in this way to make a triangular package and seal the edges with water.

6 Repeat with the remaining pastry and the remaining filling.

7 Heat the oil for deep-frying to 180–190°C/350–375°F or until a cube of bread browns in 30 seconds. Fry the samosas, in batches, for 1–2 minutes, until golden. Drain on absorbent kitchen paper and keep warm while cooking the remainder. Garnish and serve immediately.

walnut, egg & cheese pâté

serves two

1 celery stick

1–2 spring onions

25 g/1 oz shelled walnuts

1 tbsp chopped fresh parsley

1 tsp chopped fresh dill or ½ tsp
   dried dill

1 garlic clove, crushed

dash of Worcestershire sauce

115 g/4 oz cottage cheese

55 g/2 oz blue cheese, such as
   Stilton or Danish blue

1 hard-boiled egg

2 tbsp butter

salt and pepper

mixed fresh herbs, to garnish

crackers, toast or crusty bread,
   to serve

1 Finely chop the celery, slice the spring onions very thinly and chop the walnuts evenly. Put into a small mixing bowl.

2 Add the chopped herbs, garlic and Worcestershire sauce to taste and mix well. Stir the cottage cheese into the mixture and blend thoroughly.

3 Grate the blue cheese finely into the pâté mixture. Finely chop the hard-boiled egg and stir into the mixture. Season to taste with salt and pepper.

4 Melt the butter in a small pan over a low heat, then stir into the pâté. Spoon into a serving dish or 2 individual dishes. Level the top, but do not press down firmly. Chill in the refrigerator until set.

5 Garnish with mixed fresh herbs and serve with crackers, toast or fresh crusty bread.

lemon monkfish skewers

serves four

450 g/1 lb monkfish tail

2 courgettes

1 lemon

12 cherry tomatoes

8 bay leaves

BASTING SAUCE

3 tbsp olive oil

2 tbsp lemon juice

1 tsp chopped fresh thyme

½ tsp lemon pepper

salt

TO SERVE

green salad leaves

crusty bread

VARIATION

Use plaice fillets instead of the monkfish, if you prefer. Allow 2 fillets per person. Skin and cut each fillet lengthways into 2 pieces. Roll up each piece and thread them on to the skewers.

1 Cut the monkfish tail into 5-cm/2-inch chunks.

2 Cut the courgettes into thick slices and the lemon into wedges.

3 Thread the monkfish, courgettes, lemon, tomatoes and bay leaves on to 4 metal skewers.

4 To make the basting sauce, mix the oil, lemon juice, chopped thyme, lemon pepper and salt to taste together in a small bowl.

5 Brush the basting sauce liberally over the skewers. Cook the monkfish skewers on the barbecue for 15 minutes over medium-hot coals, basting them with the sauce until the fish is cooked through. Transfer to plates and serve with a green salad and crusty bread.

tuna & cheese quiche

serves four

450 g/1 lb floury potatoes, diced

2 tbsp butter

6 tbsp plain flour, plus extra
    for dusting

mixed vegetables or salad, to serve

FILLING

1 tbsp vegetable oil

1 shallot, chopped

1 garlic clove, crushed

1 red pepper, deseeded and diced

175g/6 oz drained canned tuna
    in brine

50 g/1¾ oz drained
    canned sweetcorn

150 ml/5 fl oz skimmed milk

3 eggs, beaten

1 tbsp chopped fresh dill

50 g/1¾ oz mature low-fat
    cheese, grated

salt and pepper

TO GARNISH

fresh dill sprigs

lemon wedges

1 Cook the potatoes in a large pan of boiling water for 10 minutes, or until tender.

2 Drain and mash with a fork or potato masher. Add the butter and flour and mix to form a dough.

3 Knead the potato dough on a floured surface and press into a 20-cm/8-inch flan tin. Prick the base with a fork. Line with baking paper and baking beans and bake blind in a preheated oven, 200°C/400°F/Gas Mark 6, for 20 minutes.

4 Heat the oil in a frying pan and gently cook the shallot, garlic and red pepper for 5 minutes. Spoon into the flan case. Flake the tuna and arrange in the flan with the sweetcorn.

5 In a bowl, mix the milk, eggs and chopped dill and season.

6 Pour the egg and dill mixture into the flan case and sprinkle the grated cheese on top.

7 Bake in the oven for 20 minutes, or until the filling has set. Garnish the quiche with fresh dill and lemon wedges. Serve with mixed vegetables or salad.

mini vegetable puff pastries

serves four

PASTRY CASES

450 g/1 lb puff pastry, thawed
  if frozen

1 egg, beaten

FILLING

225 g/8 oz sweet potatoes, diced

100 g/3½ oz baby asparagus spears

2 tbsp butter or margarine

1 leek, sliced

2 small open-cap mushrooms, sliced

1 tsp lime juice

1 tsp chopped fresh thyme

pinch of mustard powder

salt and pepper

COOK'S TIP

Making puff pastry yourself is
not difficult, but is immensely
time-consuming because it
involves a process of rolling,
folding and chilling that is
repeated several times. Ready-
made puff pastry, either frozen or
chilled, is usually of good quality
and is certainly more convenient
for the busy cook.

1 Cut the pastry into 4 equal pieces. Roll each piece out on a lightly floured work surface to form a 13-cm/ 5-inch square. Place on a dampened baking tray and score a smaller 6-cm/ 2½-inch square inside.

2 Brush with beaten egg and cook in a preheated oven, 200°C/ 400°F/Gas Mark 6, for 20 minutes or until risen and golden brown.

VARIATION

Use a colourful selection of any
vegetables you have to hand for
this recipe.

3 While the pastry is cooking, start the filling. Cook the sweet potato in boiling water for 15 minutes, then drain. Blanch the asparagus in boiling water for 10 minutes or until tender. Drain and reserve.

4 Remove the pastry squares from the oven. Carefully cut out the central square of pastry, lift it out and reserve.

5 Melt the butter or margarine in a pan and sauté the leek and mushrooms for 2–3 minutes. Add the lime juice, thyme and mustard, season well and stir in the sweet potatoes and asparagus. Spoon into the pastry cases, top with the reserved pastry squares and serve immediately

lamb with satay sauce

serves four

450 g/1 lb lamb loin fillet

1 tbsp mild curry paste

150 ml/5 fl oz coconut milk

2 garlic cloves, crushed

½ tsp chilli powder

½ tsp ground cumin

SATAY SAUCE

1 tbsp corn oil

1 onion, diced

6 tbsp crunchy peanut butter

1 tsp tomato purée

1 tsp fresh lime juice

100 ml/3½ fl oz water

COOK'S TIP

Soak the wooden skewers in cold water for 30 minutes before grilling to prevent the skewers from burning.

1 Using a sharp knife, thinly slice the lamb and place in a large dish.

2 Mix together the curry paste, coconut milk, garlic, chilli powder and cumin in a bowl. Pour over the lamb, toss well, cover and marinate for 30 minutes.

3 To make the satay sauce. Heat the oil in a large wok and stir-fry the onion for 5 minutes, then reduce the heat and cook for 5 minutes.

4 Stir in the peanut butter, tomato purée, lime juice and water.

5 Thread the lamb on to wooden skewers, reserving the marinade.

6 Grill the lamb skewers under a hot grill for 6–8 minutes, turning once.

7 Add the reserved marinade to the wok, bring to the boil and cook for 5 minutes. Serve the lamb skewers with the satay sauce.

crispy potato skins

serves four

8 small baking potatoes, scrubbed

4 tbsp butter, melted

salt and pepper

OPTIONAL TOPPING

6 spring onions, sliced

50 g/1¾ oz Gruyère cheese, grated

50 g/1¾ oz salami, cut into

thin strips

COOK'S TIP

Potato skins can be served on
their own, but they are delicious
served with a dip. Try a spicy
tomato or hummus dip.

1 Prick the potatoes with a fork and bake in a preheated oven, 200°C/400°F/Gas Mark 6, for about 1 hour, or until tender.

2 Cut the potatoes in half and scoop out the flesh with a teaspoon, leaving about 5-mm/¼-inch potato flesh lining the skin. Be careful not to pierce the skins.

3 Brush the insides of the potato with melted butter.

4 Place the skins, cut-side down, over medium hot coals and cook for 10–15 minutes. Alternatively, cook under a preheated grill.

5 Turn the potato skins over and cook for a further 5 minutes or until they are crispy. Take care that they do not burn.

6 Season the potato skins with salt and pepper to taste and serve while they are still warm.

7 If wished, the skins can be filled with a variety of toppings. Barbecue (or grill) the potato skins as above for about 10 minutes, then turn cut side up and sprinkle with slices of spring onion, grated cheese and salami strips. Cook on the barbecue or grill for a further 5 minutes, until the cheese begins to melt. Serve hot.

cheese, garlic & herb pâté

serves four

15 g/½ oz butter

1 garlic clove, crushed

3 spring onions, chopped finely

125 g/4½ oz full-fat soft cheese

2 tbsp chopped mixed fresh herbs,
    such as parsley, chives,
    marjoram, oregano and basil

175 g/6 oz finely grated mature
    Cheddar cheese

4–6 slices of white bread from a
    medium-cut sliced loaf

pepper

TO GARNISH

ground paprika

1 fresh flat-leaf parsley sprig

TO SERVE

mixed salad leaves

cherry tomatoes

3 Add the Cheddar cheese and work the mixture together to form a stiff paste. Cover and chill in the refrigerator until ready to serve.

4 Toast the slices of bread on both sides, then cut off the crusts. Using a sharp knife, cut through the slices horizontally to make very thin slices. Cut into triangles, then grill the untoasted sides under a preheated medium-hot grill until golden.

5 Arrange the mixed salad leaves on 4 serving plates with the cherry tomatoes. Pile the cheese pâté on top and sprinkle with a little paprika. Garnish with a fresh parsley sprig and serve with the toast.

1 Melt the butter in a large frying pan over a low heat. Add the garlic and spring onions and fry for 3–4 minutes. Leave to cool.

2 Beat the soft cheese in a large bowl until smooth, then add the garlic and spring onions. Stir in the chopped mixed herbs and mix well.

ham & cheese lattice pies

makes six

1 tbsp butter, for greasing

250 g/9 oz ready-made puff pastry,
    thawed if frozen

plain flour, for dusting

50 g/1¾ oz ham, chopped finely

125 g/4½ oz full-fat soft cheese

2 tbsp snipped fresh chives

1 egg, beaten

35 g/1¼ oz freshly grated
    Parmesan cheese

pepper

1 Grease 2 baking trays with the butter. Roll out the pastry thinly on a lightly floured work surface. Cut out 12 rectangles, each measuring 15 x 5 cm/6 x 2 inches.

2 Place the rectangles on the baking trays and chill in the refrigerator for 30 minutes.

3 Meanwhile, combine the ham, soft cheese and chives in a small bowl. Season with pepper to taste.

4 Spread the ham and cheese mixture along the centre of 6 of the rectangles, leaving a 2.5-cm/1-inch border around the edges. Brush the borders with the beaten egg.

5 To make the lattice pattern, fold the remaining rectangles lengthways. Leaving a 2.5-cm/1-inch border, cut vertical lines across the folded edge of the pastry rectangles.

6 Unfold the latticed rectangles and place them over the rectangles topped with the ham and cheese mixture. Press the edges well to seal them and lightly sprinkle the pies with the Parmesan cheese.

7 Bake in a preheated oven, 180°C/350°F/Gas Mark 4. for 15–20 minutes. Serve hot, or transfer to a wire rack to cool and serve cold.

garlic potato wedges

3 large baking potatoes, scrubbed

4 tbsp olive oil

2 tbsp butter

2 garlic cloves, chopped

1 tbsp chopped fresh rosemary

1 tbsp chopped fresh parsley

1 tbsp chopped fresh thyme

salt and pepper

COOK'S TIP

You may find it easier to barbecue these potatoes in a hinged rack.

1 Bring a large pan of water to the boil, add the potatoes and parboil them for 10 minutes. Drain the potatoes, refresh under cold water and then drain them again thoroughly.

2 Transfer the potatoes to a chopping board. When the potatoes are cold enough to handle, cut them into thick wedges, but do not peel.

3 Heat the oil and butter in a small pan together with the garlic. Cook gently until the garlic begins to brown, then remove the pan from the heat.

4 Stir the herbs and seasoning into the mixture in the pan.

5 Brush the herb and butter mixture all over the potato wedges.

6 Barbecue the potatoes over hot coals for 10–15 minutes, brushing liberally with any of the remaining herb and butter mixture, or until the potato wedges are just tender. Alternatively, cook under the grill.

7 Transfer the garlic potato wedges to a warm serving plate and serve as a starter or as a side dish.

avocado, tomato & mozzarella salad

serves four

2 tbsp pine kernels

175 g/6 oz dried fusilli

6 tomatoes

225 g/8 oz mozzarella cheese

1 large avocado pear

2 tbsp lemon juice

3 tbsp chopped fresh basil

salt and pepper

fresh basil sprigs, to garnish

DRESSING

6 tbsp extra virgin olive oil

2 tbsp white wine vinegar

1 tsp wholegrain mustard

pinch of sugar

1 Spread the pine kernels out on to a baking tray and toast under a preheated hot grill for 1–2 minutes. Remove and leave to cool.

2 Bring a large pan of lightly salted water to the boil over a medium heat. Add the pasta and cook until tender, but still firm to the bite. Drain the pasta and refresh in cold water. Drain again and leave to cool.

3 Thinly slice the tomatoes and the mozzarella cheese.

4 Using a sharp knife, cut the avocado pear in half, remove the stone and skin, then cut into thin slices lengthways. Sprinkle with lemon juice to prevent discoloration.

5 To make the dressing, whisk the oil, vinegar, mustard and sugar together in a small bowl. Season to taste with salt and pepper.

6 Arrange the sliced tomatoes, mozzarella cheese and avocado pear alternately in overlapping slices on a large serving platter.

7 Toss the pasta with half the dressing and the chopped basil and season to taste with salt and pepper. Spoon the pasta into the centre of the platter and pour over the remaining dressing. Sprinkle over the pine kernels and garnish with fresh basil sprigs. Serve immediately.

salt cod fritters

serves six

450 g/1 lb salt cod

350 g/12 oz floury baking potatoes

1 tbsp olive oil, plus extra for
  deep frying

1 onion, very finely chopped

1 garlic clove, crushed

4 tbsp very finely chopped fresh
  parsley or coriander

1 tbsp capers in brine, drained and
  chopped finely (optional)

1 small egg, lightly beaten

salt and pepper

fresh parsley, to garnish

aïoli, to serve

1 Break the salt cod into pieces and place in a bowl. Add enough water to cover and leave for 48 hours, changing the water 4 times.

2 Drain the salt cod, then cook in boiling water for 20–25 minutes, until tender. Drain, then remove all the skin and bones. Using a fork, flake the fish into fine pieces that still retain some texture.

3 Meanwhile, boil the potatoes in their skins until tender. Drain, peel and mash in a large bowl. Set aside.

4 Heat the 1 tablespoon of the oil in a frying pan. Add the onion and garlic and fry for 5 minutes, stirring, until tender but not brown. Remove with a slotted spoon and drain on kitchen paper.

5 Stir the salt cod, onion and garlic into the mashed potatoes. Stir in the parsley and capers, if using. Season generously with pepper.

6 Stir in the beaten egg. Cover and chill for 30 minutes, then adjust the seasoning.

7 Heat 5-cm/2-inch of oil in a deep fryer to 180–190°C/350–375°F, or until a cube of bread browns in 30 seconds. Drop tablespoonfuls of the salt-cod mixture into the hot oil and fry for about 8 minutes, or until golden brown and set. Do not fry more than 6 at a time because the oil will become too cold and the fritters will become soggy. You will get 18–20 fritters.

8 Drain the fritters on kitchen paper. Serve at once with aïoli for dipping. Garnish with parsley.

tortelloni

makes thirty-six pieces

about 300 g/10½ oz thin sheets
    of fresh pasta

75 g/2¾ oz butter

50 g/1¾ oz shallots, chopped finely

3 garlic cloves, crushed

50 g/1¾ oz mushrooms, wiped and
    chopped finely

½ celery stick, chopped finely

25 g/1 oz freshly grated pecorino
    cheese, plus extra to garnish

1 tbsp oil

salt and pepper

1 Using a serrated pasta cutter, cut 5-cm/2-inch squares from the sheets of fresh pasta. To make 36 tortelloni, you will need 72 squares. Once the pasta is cut, cover the squares with clingfilm to stop them drying out.

2 Heat 25 g/1 oz of the butter in a frying pan over a low heat. Add the shallots, 1 crushed garlic clove, mushrooms and celery and cook for 4–5 minutes.

3 Remove the pan from the heat, stir in the cheese and season to taste with salt and pepper.

4 Spoon ½ teaspoon of the mixture on to the centre of 36 pasta squares. Brush the edges with water and top with the remaining 36 squares. Press the edges together to seal. Leave to rest for 5 minutes.

5 Bring a large pan of water to the boil over a medium heat. Add the oil and cook the tortelloni, in batches, for 2–3 minutes. The tortelloni will rise to the surface when cooked and the pasta should be tender with a slight bite. Remove from the pan with a slotted spoon and drain thoroughly.

6 Meanwhile, melt the remaining butter in a pan over a low heat. Add the remaining garlic and plenty of pepper and cook for 1–2 minutes.

7 Transfer the tortelloni to 4 serving plates and pour over the garlic butter. Garnish with grated pecorino cheese and serve immediately.

pissaladière

serves eight

1 tbsp butter, for greasing

4 tbsp olive oil

700 g/1 lb 9 oz red onions,
    sliced thinly

2 garlic cloves, crushed

2 tsp caster sugar

2 tbsp red wine vinegar

salt and pepper

plain flour, for dusting

350 g/12 oz ready-made puff
    pastry, thawed if frozen

TOPPING

100 g/3½ oz canned anchovy fillets

12 stoned green olives

1 tsp dried marjoram

VARIATION

Cut the pissaladière into squares
or triangles for easy finger food
at a party or barbecue.

---

1 Lightly grease a Swiss roll tin with butter. Heat the oil in a large, heavy-based saucepan. Add the onions and garlic and cook over a low heat for about 30 minutes, stirring occasionally.

2 Add the sugar and red wine vinegar to the saucepan and season with plenty of salt and pepper.

3 On a lightly floured surface, roll out the pastry to a rectangle measuring 33 x 23 cm/13 x 9 inches. Place the pastry rectangle in the prepared tin, pushing the pastry well into the corners of the tin.

4 Spread the onion mixture evenly over the pastry.

5 To make the decorative topping, arrange the anchovy fillets in a criss-cross pattern on top of the onion mixture, place the green olives in between the anchovies, then sprinkle the marjoram over the top.

6 Bake in a preheated oven, 220°C/425°F/Gas Mark 7, for 20–25 minutes, until the pissaladière is lightly golden. Serve piping hot, straight from the oven.

mini pizzas

serves eight

BASIC PIZZA DOUGH

2 tsp dried yeast

1 tsp sugar

250 ml/9 fl oz hand-hot water

350 g/12 oz strong plain flour, plus
    extra for dusting

1 tsp salt

1 tbsp olive oil, plus extra
    for brushing

TOPPING

2 courgettes

100 ml/3½ fl oz passata

75 g/2¾ oz pancetta, diced

50 g/1¾ oz black olives, stoned
    and chopped

1 tbsp mixed dried herbs

2 tbsp olive oil

salt and pepper

1 To make the dough, mix the yeast and sugar with 4 tablespoons of the water in a bowl. Leave in a warm place for 15 minutes or until frothy.

2 In a separate bowl, mix the flour with the salt and make a well in the centre. Add the oil, yeast mixture and remaining water. Mix into a smooth dough using a wooden spoon.

3 Turn the dough out on to a floured work surface and knead for 4–5 minutes, or until smooth. Return the dough to the mixing bowl, cover with an oiled sheet of clingfilm and leave in a warm place to rise for 30 minutes, or until the dough has doubled in size.

4 Knead the dough for 2 minutes, then divide it into 8 balls. Roll out each portion thinly to form a round about 10 cm/4 inches wide, then place the 8 dough rounds on an oiled baking tray and push out the edges until even. The dough should be no more than 5 mm/¼ inch thick because it will rise during cooking.

5 To make the topping, grate the courgettes finely. Cover them with absorbent kitchen paper and leave to stand for about 10 minutes to soak up some of the juices.

6 Spread 2–3 teaspoons of the passata over each pizza base and top with the grated courgettes, pancetta and olives. Season with pepper and add a sprinkling of mixed dried herbs to taste, then drizzle with olive oil.

7 Bake in a preheated oven, 200°C/400°F/Gas Mark 6, for 15 minutes, or until crispy. Season to taste and serve hot.

garlic & sage bread

serves six

1 tbsp vegan margarine,
    for greasing
250 g/9 oz strong brown
    bread flour
1 sachet easy-blend dried yeast
3 tbsp chopped fresh sage
2 tsp sea salt
3 garlic cloves, chopped finely
1 tsp clear honey
150 ml/5 fl oz hand-hot water

1 Grease a baking tray with the margarine. Sieve the flour into a large mixing bowl and add any bran remaining in the sieve.

2 Stir in the dried yeast, chopped sage and half of the sea salt. Reserve 1 teaspoon of the chopped garlic for sprinkling and stir the remainder into the bowl. Add the honey and water and bring together to form a dough.

3 Turn the dough out on to a lightly floured work surface and knead it for about 5 minutes. Alternatively, use an electric mixer with a dough hook.

4 Place the dough in a greased bowl, cover and leave to rise in a warm place until doubled in size.

5 Knead the dough for a few minutes to knock it back, shape it into a ring (see Cook's Tip) and place on the baking tray.

6 Cover and leave to rise for a further 30 minutes, or until springy to the touch. Sprinkle with the rest of the sea salt and garlic.

7 Bake the loaf in a preheated oven, 200°C/400°F/Gas Mark 6, for 25–30 minutes. Transfer to a wire rack to cool before serving.

COOK'S TIP

Roll the dough into a long
sausage and then curve it into
a circular shape. You can omit
the sea salt for sprinkling,
if you wish.

65

cheese sablés

makes thirty-five

150 g/5½ oz butter, diced, plus
    extra for greasing
150 g/5½ oz plain flour, plus extra
    for dusting
150 g/5½ oz mature cheese, grated
1 egg yolk
sesame seeds, for sprinkling

COOK'S TIP

Cut out any shape you like for
your savoury biscuits. Children
will enjoy them cut into animal
shapes or other fun designs.

1 Lightly grease several baking trays
with a little butter.

2 Mix the flour and cheese together
in a bowl.

3 Add the butter to the cheese
and flour mixture and rub in with
your fingertips until the mixture
resembles breadcrumbs.

4 Stir in the egg yolk and mix to
form a dough. Wrap in clingfilm.
Chill in the refrigerator for 30 minutes.

5 Roll out the dough thinly on a
lightly floured work surface.
Stamp out rounds with a 6-cm/2½-inch
biscuit cutter, re-rolling the trimmings
to make 35 biscuits.

6 Place the rounds on to the
prepared baking trays and
sprinkle the sesame seeds over the
top of them.

7 Bake in a preheated oven,
200°C/400°F/Gas Mark 6, for
20 minutes, until lightly golden.

8 Carefully transfer the cheese
sablés to a wire rack and leave
to cool slightly before serving.

VARIATION

For a sweet variation of these
traditional French biscuits,
substitute the grated rind of
1 lemon for the cheese and stir in
125 g/4½ oz caster sugar at the
end of step 2. Beat the egg yolk
with 1 tablespoon brandy or rum
before adding it to the mixture.
Roll out the dough, stamp out
rounds and bake as above.

sun-dried tomato loaf

serves four

10 g/¼ oz dried yeast

1 tsp granulated sugar

300 ml/10 fl oz hand-hot water

450 g/1 lb strong white flour, plus
    extra for dusting

1 tsp salt

2 tsp dried basil

2 tbsp sun-dried tomato paste or
    tomato purée

1 tbsp vegan margarine,
    for greasing

12 sun-dried tomatoes in oil,
    drained and cut into strips

1 Place the yeast and sugar in a bowl. Mix with 100 ml/3½ fl oz of the water. Leave in a warm place for about 15 minutes, or until frothy.

2 Mix the flour and salt together in a large bowl. Make a well in the dry ingredients and add the basil, yeast mixture, tomato paste and half of the remaining water. Draw the flour into the liquid with a wooden spoon and bring together to form a dough, adding the rest of the water a little at a time.

3 Turn the dough out on to a lightly floured work surface and knead for 5 minutes, or until smooth. Cover with oiled clingfilm and leave in a warm place to rise for about 30 minutes, or until doubled in size.

4 Lightly grease a 900-g/2-lb loaf tin with the margarine.

5 Turn the dough out and knead in the sun-dried tomatoes. Knead for a further 2–3 minutes.

6 Place the dough in the prepared loaf tin and leave to rise for 30–40 minutes. or until doubled in size again. Bake the loaf in a preheated oven, 190°C/375°F/Gas Mark 5, for 30–35 minutes, or until golden. When the loaf is cooked, it should sound hollow when tapped on the base. Cool slightly on a wire rack and serve.

mini focaccia

serves four

2 tbsp olive oil, plus extra
for greasing

350 g/12 oz strong white flour, plus
extra for dusting

½ tsp salt

1 sachet easy-blend dried yeast

250 ml/9 fl oz hand-hot water

100 g/3½ oz stoned green or black
olives, halved

TOPPING

2 red onions, sliced

2 tbsp olive oil

1 tsp sea salt

1 tbsp thyme leaves

1 Lightly oil several baking trays.
Sieve the flour and salt into a
large mixing bowl, then stir in the
yeast. Pour in the olive oil and water
and bring together with your fingers
to form a dough.

2 Turn the dough out on to a lightly
floured work surface and knead
for about 5 minutes. Alternatively, use
an electric mixer with a dough hook.

3 Place the dough in a greased
bowl, cover and leave in a warm
place for about 1–1½ hours, or until it
has doubled in size.

4 Knead the dough for 1–2 minutes
to knock it back, then knead half
of the olives into the dough. Divide the
dough into quarters, then shape the
quarters into rounds. Place them on
the baking trays and push your fingers
into the dough rounds to create a
dimpled effect.

5 To make the topping, sprinkle the
red onions and remaining olives
over the rounds. Drizzle the oil over the
top and sprinkle with the sea salt and
thyme leaves. Cover and leave to rise
for 30 minutes.

6 Bake in a preheated oven,
190°C/375°F/Gas Mark 5, for
20–25 minutes, or until the focaccia
are golden.

7 Transfer to a wire rack and leave
to cool before serving.

VARIATION

Use this quantity of dough
to make 1 large focaccia,
if you wish.

69

garlic bread rolls

makes eight

1 tbsp butter, for greasing

12 cloves garlic,

350 ml/12 fl oz milk, plus extra
for brushing

450 g/1 lb strong white bread flour,
plus extra for dusting

1 tsp salt

1 sachet easy-blend dried yeast

1 tbsp dried mixed herbs

2 tbsp sunflower oil

1 egg, beaten

milk, for brushing

rock salt, for sprinkling

1 Lightly grease a baking tray with the butter.

2 Peel the garlic cloves and place them in a saucepan with the milk. Bring to the boil and simmer gently over a low heat for 15 minutes. Leave to cool slightly, then place in a food processor and process into a purée.

3 Sieve the flour and salt into a large mixing bowl and stir in the dried yeast and mixed herbs.

4 Add the garlic-flavoured milk, sunflower oil and beaten egg to the dry ingredients, then mix well and bring together with your fingers to form a dough.

5 Turn the dough out on to a lightly floured work surface and knead lightly for a few minutes until smooth and soft.

6 Place the dough in a lightly greased bowl, cover and leave to rise in a warm place for about 1 hour, or until doubled in size.

7 Knead the dough for 2 minutes to knock it back. Divide into 8 rolls and place on the prepared baking tray. Score the top of each roll with a knife, cover and leave for 15 minutes.

8 Brush the rolls with milk and sprinkle rock salt over the top.

9 Bake in a preheated oven, 220°C/425°F/Gas Mark 7, for 15–20 minutes. Transfer to a wire rack and leave to cool before serving.

spiced biscuits

makes twelve

175 g/6 oz unsalted butter, plus
   extra for greasing
175 g/6 oz dark muscovado sugar
225 g/8 oz plain flour
a pinch of salt
½ tsp bicarbonate of soda
1 tsp ground cinnamon
½ tsp ground coriander
½ tsp ground nutmeg
¼ tsp ground cloves
2 tbsp dark rum

1 Lightly grease 2 baking trays with
a little butter.

2 Cream the butter and sugar
together in a mixing bowl until
light and fluffy.

3 Sieve the flour, salt, bicarbonate
of soda, cinnamon, coriander,
nutmeg and cloves into the butter and
sugar mixture.

COOK'S TIP

Use the back of a fork to flatten
the biscuits instead of a spoon,
to give them a textured surface.

4 Stir the dark rum into the creamed
mixture until blended.

5 Place 12 small mounds of the
mixture on to the baking trays
using 2 teaspoons. Space the mounds
well apart to allow room to expand
during cooking. Flatten each one
slightly with the back of a spoon.

6 Bake in a preheated oven,
180°C/350°F/Gas Mark 4, for
10–12 minutes, until golden.

7 Carefully transfer the biscuits to
wire racks to cool completely and
crisp before serving.

cannoli

makes twenty

3 tbsp lemon juice

3 tbsp water

1 large egg

250 g/9 oz plain flour

1 tbsp caster sugar

1 tsp ground mixed spice

pinch of salt

25 g/1 oz butter, softened

sunflower oil, for deep-frying

1 small egg white, beaten lightly

icing sugar

FILLING

750 g/1 lb 10 oz ricotta cheese,
    drained

4 tbsp icing sugar

1 tsp vanilla essence

finely grated rind of 1 large orange

4 tbsp very finely chopped candied
    peel

50 g/1¾ oz plain chocolate, grated

pinch of ground cinnamon

2 tbsp Marsala wine or orange juice

1 Combine the lemon juice, water and egg. Put the flour, sugar, spice and salt into a food processor and quickly process. Add the butter, then with the motor running, pour the egg mixture through the feed tube. Process until the mixture just forms a dough.

2 Turn the dough out on to a lightly floured surface and knead lightly. Wrap and chill for at least 1 hour.

3 Meanwhile, make the filling. Beat the ricotta cheese until smooth. Sift in the icing sugar, then beat in the remaining ingredients. Cover with clingfilm and chill until required.

4 Roll out the dough on a floured surface until 2 mm/¹⁄₁₆-inch thick. Using a ruler, cut out 8.5 x 7.5-cm/ 3½ x 3-inch pieces, re-rolling and cutting the trimmings, making about 20 pieces in all.

5 Heat 5 cm/2 inches of oil in a deep, heavy-based frying pan to 190°C/375°F. Roll a piece of pastry around a greased cannoli mould, to just overlap the edge. Seal with egg white, pressing firmly. Repeat with all the moulds you have. Deep-fry 2 or 3 moulds until the cannoli are golden, crisp and bubbly.

6 Remove the cannoli with a slotted spoon and drain on kitchen paper. Leave until cool, then carefully slide them off the moulds. Repeat with the remaining cannoli.

7 Store unfilled in an airtight container for up to 2 days. Pipe in the filling no more than 30 minutes before serving to prevent the pastry becoming soggy. Sift icing sugar over the cannoli and serve.

meringue creams

makes thirteen

4 egg whites

pinch of salt

125 g/4½ oz granulated sugar

125 g/4½ oz caster sugar

300 ml/10 fl oz double cream,
    whipped lightly, to serve

VARIATION

For a finer texture, replace
the granulated sugar with
caster sugar.

1 Line 3 large baking trays with
baking paper.

2 Whisk the egg whites and salt
together in a large bowl until they
are stiff, using an electric whisk or a
balloon whisk. (You should be able to
turn the bowl upside down without
any movement from the egg whites.)

3 Whisk in the granulated sugar,
a little at a time; the meringue
should start to look glossy.

4 Whisk in the caster sugar, a little
at a time, whisking well after
each addition until all the sugar has
been incorporated and the meringue is
thick, white and forms peaks.

5 Transfer the meringue mixture
into a piping bag fitted with a
2-cm/¾-inch star nozzle. Pipe about
26 small whirls of meringue on to the
prepared baking trays.

6 Bake in a preheated oven, 120°C/
250°F/Gas Mark ½, for 1½ hours,
or until the meringues are pale golden
and can be easily lifted off the paper.
Turn off the heat and leave them to
cool in the oven overnight.

7 Just before serving, sandwich
the meringue whirls together in
pairs with the cream and arrange on
a serving plate.

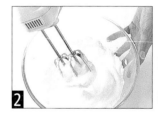

hazelnut squares

makes sixteen

100 g/3½ oz butter, diced, plus
extra for greasing

150 g/5½ oz plain flour

pinch of salt

1 tsp baking powder

150 g/5½ oz soft brown sugar

1 egg, beaten

4 tbsp milk

100 g/3½ oz hazelnuts, halved

demerara sugar, for
sprinkling (optional)

1 Grease a 23-cm/9-inch square cake tin with a little butter and line the base with baking paper.

2 Sieve the flour, salt and baking powder into a large mixing bowl.

3 Add the butter and rub in with your fingertips until the mixture resembles fine breadcrumbs. Add the soft brown sugar to the mixture and stir to blend.

4 Add the beaten egg, milk and halved hazelnuts to the dry ingredients and stir well until thoroughly blended and the mixture has a soft consistency.

5 Spoon the mixture into the prepared cake tin and level the surface with a palette knife. Sprinkle with demerara sugar, if you wish.

VARIATION

For a coffee time biscuit, replace the milk with the same amount of cold strong black coffee – the stronger the better!

6 Bake in a preheated oven, 180°C/ 350°F/Gas Mark 4, for about 25 minutes, or until the surface is firm to the touch.

7 Leave to cool in the tin for about 10 minutes, then loosen the edges with a palette knife and turn out on to a wire rack. Cut into 16 squares to serve.

chocolate mascarpone cups

makes twenty

100 g/3½ oz plain chocolate

FILLING

100 g/3½ oz milk or plain chocolate

200 g/7 oz mascarpone cheese

¼ tsp vanilla essence

cocoa powder, for dusting

VARIATION

Substitute full-fat crème fraîche for mascarpone cheese. Its delicate flavour blends well with chocolate.

2 When set, carefully peel away the paper cases.

1 Line a baking tray with a sheet of baking paper. Break 100 g/3½ oz plain chocolate into pieces, place in a bowl and set over a saucepan of hot water. Stir until the chocolate has melted. Spoon the melted chocolate into 20 paper sweet cases, spreading up the sides with a small spoon or pastry brush. Place upside down on the baking tray and leave to set.

3 For the filling, melt the chocolate. Place the mascarpone cheese in a bowl and beat in the vanilla essence and melted chocolate until well combined. Leave the mixture to chill in the refrigerator, beating occasionally, until firm enough to pipe.

4 Place the mascarpone filling in a piping bag fitted with a star nozzle and pipe the mixture into the cups. Decorate the cups with a dusting of cocoa powder.

collettes

makes twenty

100 g/3½ oz white chocolate

FILLING

150 g/5½ oz orange-flavoured
   plain chocolate

150 ml/5 fl oz double cream

2 tbsp icing sugar

COOK'S TIP

If they do not hold their
shape well, use 2 cases to
make a double thickness mould.
Foil cases are firmer, so use
these if you can find them.

1 Line a baking tray with a sheet of baking paper. Break the chocolate into pieces, place in a bowl and set over a saucepan of hot water. Stir until melted, and spoon into 20 paper sweet cases, spreading up the sides with a small pastry brush. Place upside down on the prepared baking tray and leave to set.

2 When set, carefully peel away the paper cases.

3 To make the filling, melt the orange-flavoured chocolate and place in a mixing bowl with the cream and the icing sugar. Beat the chocolate cream until smooth. Chill until the mixture becomes firm enough to pipe, stirring occasionally.

4 Place the filling in a piping bag fitted with a star nozzle and pipe a little into each case. Leave to chill until required.

This is a Parragon Book
This edition published in 2004

Parragon
Queen Street House
4 Queen Street
Bath BA1 1HE, UK

ISBN: 1-40544-090-2

Printed in China
Produced by the Bridgewater Company Ltd

NOTE

This book also uses imperial and metric measurements. Follow the same units
of measurement throughout; do not mix imperial and metric.
All spoon measurements are level: teaspoons are assumed to be 5 ml and
tablespoons are assumed to be 15 ml. Unless otherwise stated, milk is assumed
to be whole milk, eggs and individual vegetables such as potatoes are medium,
and pepper is freshly ground black pepper.

The times given for each recipe are an approximate guide only because the
preparation times may differ according to the techniques used by different
people and the cooking times may vary as a result of the type of oven used.

Recipes using raw or very lightly cooked eggs should be
avoided by infants, the elderly, pregnant women, convalescents, and anyone
suffering from an illness.